The Transatlantic Slave Trade: The History an
Brought Slaves to the New ...

By Charles River Editors

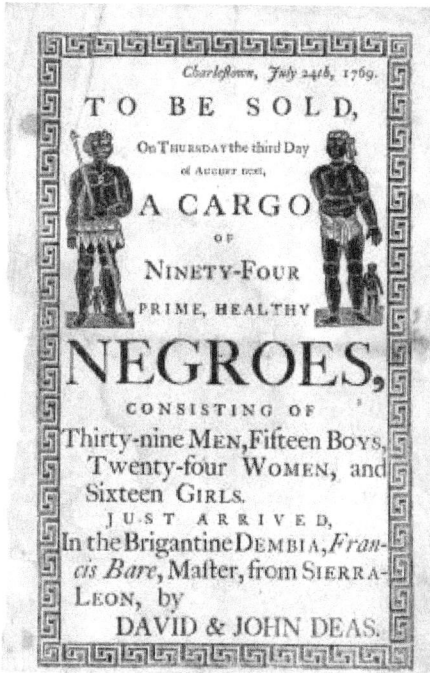

Charlestown, July 24th, 1769.

TO BE SOLD,

On THURSDAY the third Day
of AUGUST next,

A CARGO

OF

NINETY-FOUR

PRIME, HEALTHY

NEGROES,

CONSISTING OF

Thirty-nine MEN, Fifteen BOYS,
Twenty-four WOMEN, and
Sixteen GIRLS.
JUST ARRIVED,
In the Brigantine DEMBIA, *Fran-
cis Bare*, Master, from SIERRA-
LEON, by
DAVID & JOHN DEAS.

Picture of an advertisement

About Charles River Editors

Charles River Editors provides superior editing and original writing services in the digital publishing industry, with the expertise to create digital content for publishers across a vast range of subject matter. In addition to providing original digital content for third party publishers, we also republish civilization's greatest literary works, bringing them to new generations of readers via ebooks.

Introduction

"The Slave Trade" by Auguste François Biard (1840)

The Transatlantic Slave Trade

"The deck, that is the floor of their rooms, was so covered with the blood and mucus which had proceeded from them in consequence of the flux, that it resembled a slaughter-house. It is not in the power of the human imagination to picture a situation more dreadful or disgusting. Numbers of the slaves having fainted, they were carried upon deck where several of them died and the rest with great difficulty were restored. It had nearly proved fatal to me also." – Dr. Alexander Falconbridge, an 18th century British surgeon

It has often been said that the greatest invention of all time was the sail, which facilitated the internationalization of the globe and thus ushered in the modern era. Columbus' contact with the New World, alongside European maritime contact with the Far East, transformed human history, and in particular the history of Africa.

It was the sail that linked the continents of Africa and America, and thus it was also the sail that facilitated the greatest involuntary human migration of all time. The African slave trade is a complex and deeply divisive subject that has had a tendency to evolve according the political requirements of any given age, and is often touchable only with the correct distribution of culpability. It has for many years, therefore, been deemed singularly unpalatable to implicate Africans themselves in the perpetration of the institution, and only in recent years has the large-scale African involvement in both the Atlantic and Indian Ocean Slave Trades come to be an accepted fact. There can, however, be no doubt that even though large numbers of indigenous Africans were liable, it was European ingenuity and greed that fundamentally drove the industrialization of the Transatlantic slave trade in response to massive new market demands created by their equally ruthless exploitation of the Americas.

In time, the Atlantic slave trade provided for the labor requirements of the emerging plantation economies of the New World. It was a specific, dedicated and industrial enterprise wherein huge profits were at stake, and a vast and highly organized network of procurement, processing, transport and sale existed to expedite what was in effect a modern commodity market. It existed without sentimentality, without history, and without tradition, and it was only outlawed once the advances of the industrial revolution had created alternative sources of energy for agricultural production.

The Transatlantic Slave Trade: The History and Legacy of the System that Brought Slaves to the New World looks at the notorious trade network. Along with pictures of important people, places, and events, you will learn about the Transatlantic slave trade like never before, in no time at all.

The Transatlantic Slave Trade: The History and Legacy of the System that Brought Slaves to the New World

Chapter 1: The Origins of the Atlantic Slave Trade

If it was the sail that united the world and made possible the phenomena of European global expansion and the commercial exploitation of the tropics, it was sugar, tobacco and cotton that provided the economic catalyst. The discovery of the New World, and specifically of climatic conditions ideal for the large-scale production of these commodities, triggered an immediate and increasing demand for cheap labor. Initially local indigenous populations were exploited in this regard, but very quickly this policy proved itself to be unsustainable. Thereafter, attempts to import voluntary European manpower was tried, followed by indentured or convict labor, but neither offered the sort of numbers necessary to maximize profits. It quickly became evident that only slavery or some other form of coerced labor would offer a practical solution to the economic emergence of the New World.

The question of where sufficient quantities of slave labor could be acquired was answered fairly quickly by a growing commercial intimacy between Europe and the west coast of Africa. The internal slave trade in Europe had long since ceased, for obvious moral and practical reasons, but black Africans were not at that point included in the emerging European social contract, and where therefore deemed eligible to be enslaved. On top of that, the Europeans believed Africans were relatively easy to acquire, were physically superior, were resistant to pernicious disease, and were well adapted to labor in the tropics.

Since the fall of Constantinople in the mid-15th century, Portugal had begun to exploit its position at the edge of the Atlantic to set out to largely unmapped territories in search of new routes, new resources, and ultimately, a new path to the East that would circumvent the Ottoman blockade. But even prior to conceiving that goal, the Portuguese had been at the vanguard of oceanic exploration, and by the 1420s had already arrived at and established settlements on the Atlantic islands of Madeira and the Azores. The intellectual architect of Portuguese exploration was Prince Henry the Navigator, who was motivated by religious zeal to send expeditions down the Atlantic coast of Africa, initially hoping to check Muslim power on the continent and make contact with Prester John, a legendary Christian king in Africa (the legend was probably a garbled version of the Christian kingdom of Ethiopia). In the decades prior to Columbus's arrival in Lisbon, Portuguese expeditions had pushed farther and farther southward down the West African coast, opening up new trade in gold, ivory, and African slaves along the way. By the 1450s, the goal of circumnavigating Africa to reach Asia had been conceived.

Henry the Navigator

Furthermore, the Portuguese were being strongly encouraged by the Catholic Church. In the 1450s, the Pope issued papal bulls promising Portugal that at least among Catholic nations, Portugal would be given a trade monopoly in lands they discovered in Africa south of the Sahara. That was all the motivation the Portuguese needed: by then, the Portuguese had already sailed to Sierra Leone, on the western coast of Africa about half of the way down the continent. And in 1488, the Portuguese explorer Bartolomeu Dias became the first European to sail around the Cape of Good Hope, discovering much to his amazement that the Indian Ocean was connected to the Atlantic Ocean. One of the missions of Dias' expedition was to sail to India, which was a stated objective despite the fact the Portuguese did not realize they could sail around Africa to Asia. Dias did not reach India, but in 1497, Portugal's most famous explorer, Vasco da Gama sailed around Cape Good Hope, sailed north up the eastern coast of Africa and then sailed to Calicut, India, arriving in 1498.

Christopher Columbus would find the New World by promoting a different route than that sought by the Portuguese, but the Portuguese explorers and traders had prepared the way for his ideas in several ways. First, the increasing confidence about long-distance sea travel, based in part on improved nautical technology and cartographical accuracy, made the notion of connecting distant regions by sea far more plausible than it had been even a hundred years earlier. For much of the Middle Ages, it was assumed that any routes connecting Europe and Asia would be land routes. Medieval cartography had always shown the possibility of sea routes, since they showed the three known continents of Europe, Asia, and Africa to be surrounded by a continuous body of water, but sea travel was regarded as far too dangerous and untested. The Portuguese explorations of the 15th century began to make this conviction look like an unfounded prejudice.

A second obstacle had been the belief, held since ancient times, that the Southern hemisphere was an uninhabitable torrid zone where life could not thrive. Now the Portuguese had traveled much farther to the south than any Europeans before them and had found the climate pleasant, the vegetation abundant, and the ground rich in mineral deposits. These discoveries found confirmation in the rediscovered work of the ancient Greek geographer Ptolemy, who had painted a relatively pleasant picture of the tropical zones of Africa. In fact, the Portuguese would find so many inhabitants of Africa that when the Pope issued his papal bulls granting the Portuguese a trade monopoly in lands they discovered in south Africa, he gave the Portuguese the "right" to make "Saracens, pagans and any other unbelievers" slaves.

The first African slaves to be transported across the Atlantic were in fact sourced from Europe itself, but very quickly trade links began to be established along the west coast of Africa for the specific purpose of sourcing slave labor. This relationship was initially pioneered by the Portuguese, but soon enough all of the major European powers had begun to adapt their international trade practices to the lucrative triangular trade in slaves, setting the pattern for the next three centuries or more of ruthless exploitation.

It is interesting to note that at this pivotal moment – the mid-16th century – the west coast of Africa itself was sufficiently strong to resistant any attempts that might have been made by the Europeans to physically establish themselves on the African mainland, and there to build the same economic infrastructure that was underway in the Americas. Climate played a part in this, but primarily it was a powerful African establishment protecting its shores and its trade interests that prevented the Europeans from making substantial landfall. For the Europeans, it ultimately proved itself to be more economical to simply exploit and profit from the willingness of powerful indigenous entities on the African mainland to trade not only their natural commodities but also their human resources.

Towards the end of the 15th century, the British, French and to a lesser extent the Dutch entered the race to explore and chart the globe, and by extension to claim portions of it in advance of their own maritime trade. Among the great discoveries of this period were Australia in 1606, New Zealand in 1642, and Hawaii in 1778. Ultimately, however, credit for establishing the first roots of European trade along the west coast of Africa belongs to the Portuguese. The first Portuguese factory and trading post were located on the island of Arguin, located just off the coast of Mauritania, followed by a steady expansion southwards towards the coasts of Gambia and Senegal. Initial trade was limited and tended to be confined to gold, pepper and ivory, with a very limited movement of slaves supplying sugar plantations in the Mediterranean, and later

Madeira. It was the Portuguese colonization of Brazil in the 16th century, however, and the establishment of commercial sugar plantations that precipitated the movement of slaves directly from West Africa to the New World, and it would be from this basis that the Transatlantic slave trade would develop.

An illustration depicting Portuguese traders in Africa

A depiction of slaves in Brazil

The first organized trading enterprise to begin operations in West Africa was a Portuguese chartered company, the *Company of Guinea*, which was established in 1482. This was followed in due time by a number of similar European companies that established and retained close trading relationships with dominant indigenous interests on the mainland. In time, the slave trade became inextricably intertwined with the emergence and activities of these chartered companies, which were simply early commercial associations formed by investors or shareholders for the purpose of foreign trade, exploration and later colonization. Chartered companies in one form or another would be highly influential in the occupation and colonization of Africa, particularly during the latter half of the 19th century. Arguably the most influential and best known chartered company was the British East India Company, which was founded in 1591 and which later occupied and governed much of India before the establishment of the British Raj in 1858.

The legitimacy and authorization of such private companies were granted under a royal charter, or in the case of a republic, a government charter. This charter typically defined the terms under which a company could trade, and also the extent to which it could administer and exercise authority over a given area of territory. Chartered companies were responsible for the establishment of some of the larger territorial blocs in Africa. For example, the Royal Niger Company laid the groundwork for what would later become Nigeria, the Royal East Africa Company did the same for the territories of Kenya and Uganda, and the British South Africa Company helped establish Zimbabwe and Zambia. There were many others besides, and Dutch, Swedish, Danish, British, French and Portuguese companies all vied for domination of the most lucrative trade regions along the west coast of Africa. Influential trading entrepôt emerged in such places as Gorée Island, adjacent to Dakar (the modern day capital of Senegal), as well as on Bonny island in the Bight of Benin, Whydah on the coast of modern Benin. Perhaps the greatest concentration of influence was exerted along the coast of modern day Ghana, then known broadly as the Slave Coast.

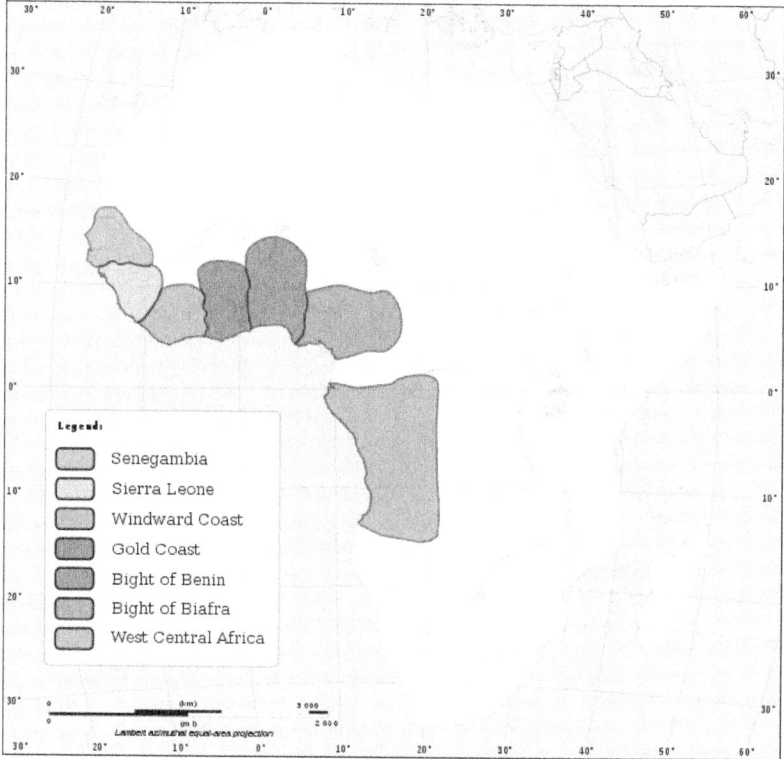

A map of major trading territories along the coast

A depiction of slave traders in Goree

In Ghana today, the remnants of a number of old slaving forts and factories survive, with perhaps the most famous (or infamous) being Christiansborg (now Osu Castle), Cape Coast Castle and Elmina. All three of them remain sobering monuments to centuries of human traffic in the region.

Osu Castle, originally Christiansborg Castle, was named after the Danish King Christian V. The region was dominated by the Danes from the 1660s, when the castle was taken over from *The Swedish Africa Company*, until 1850 when all of Denmark's trading interests on the Gold and Slave Coasts were sold to the British. It was the Danes, however, who were the first to use the site as a base for the processing and shipment of slaves, and indeed , Christiansborg, Cape Coast and Elmina castles each evolved for the specific purpose of housing, processing and embarking slaves on ships destined for the New World.

A contemporary illustration of Christiansborg Castle

These sites, and others besides, were in practical use for centuries, passing between the principal trading powers frequently as a consequence of purchase and conquest. In the modern era, a handful of these sites have been preserved (including some as UNESCO International Heritage Sites), although many others have fallen into ruin, and have largely disappeared.

Thus, this is how the origins of the system coalesced into the network initially. European trading powers (Portuguese, Spanish, British, French, Swedish, Danish and Dutch) established their various spheres of influence along the west coast of Africa, forging links with dominant local trading powers, trading initially in a wide range of products and commodities but specializing more and more as time went by in the trade in slaves.

INSPECTION AND SALE OF A NEGRO.

An illustration depicting the inspection and sale of slaves

The Atlantic slave trade has tended to be divided into two eras known as the First and Second Atlantic Systems. The First Atlantic System, under the control of the Spanish and the Portuguese, marked the early movement of African slaves from the African mainland to South America and the various Portuguese and Spanish colonies. This phase of the trade was slow to start, and it only began to reach a significant scale after 1500. In 1562, Captain John Hawkins became the first English captain to voyage to Africa and acquire slaves on behalf of British interests. Over the next several years, Hawkins made a number of voyages and took about 1,200 slaves, which were subsequently sold in the Americas. That said, it remained almost entirely in Portuguese hands for that period, with only a handful of British, French and Dutch traders able to challenge the Portuguese monopoly.

Hawkins

By the beginning of the 17th century, however, the influence of the British, French and Dutch began to exceed that of the Portuguese, in particular once slave markets had been established throughout the New World (especially the Caribbean and North America). The main destination of exported slaves then became the Caribbean and Brazil, with British North America accounting only for a minimal five percent of all slaves arriving in the New World.

During the initial phases of British involvement, traders supplied slaves for the Spanish and Portuguese colonists in America. However, as British settlements in the Caribbean and North America grew, often through wars with European countries such as Holland, Spain and France, British slave traders increasingly supplied British colonies. The first record of enslaved Africans being landed in the British colony of Virginia was in 1619. Barbados became the first British settlement in the Caribbean in 1625, and the British took control of Jamaica in 1655. •   British involvement in the trans-Atlantic Slave Trade expanded rapidly in response to the demand for labor on the sugar plantations of Barbados and other British West Indian islands. By the 1660s, the number of slaves exported from Africa in British ships was averaging about 6,700 per year. A century later, Britain had become the leading European nation implicated in the trans-Atlantic Slave Trade. Of the 80,000 or so Africans transported across the Atlantic on an annual basis, 42,000 were carried by British slave ships.

A depiction of slaves harvesting tobacco in Virginia in the 17th century

By the 18th century, the Dutch, Danes and Swedes had more or less dropped out of the trade, leaving British, French and Portuguese carriers responsible for upwards of 90 percent of slave traffic. This was the Second Atlantic System, and it has been estimated that more than half of the entire volume of slave traffic was accounted for during this period, which was dominated by the English who ultimately would rank first among nations implicated in the trans-Atlantic Slave Trade. Slavery remained a legal institution in all of the 13 American colonies and Canada, the latter acquired by Britain in 1763. At the time of the Industrial Revolution, profits from the Slave Trade and from the British West Indian plantations amounted to a full 5 percent of the overall British economy.

In the 245 years between Captain John Hawkins' first voyage and the abolition of the Slave Trade in 1807, merchants in Britain accounted for about 10,000 individual voyages to Africa for slaves, with merchants in other parts of the British Empire perhaps fitting out a further 1,150 voyages. Historian, Professor David Richardson, has calculated that British ships carried 3.4 million or more enslaved Africans to the Americas. This was exceeded only by the Portuguese, who continued to trade slaves across the Atlantic for almost 50 years after Britain had abolished the trade. Rough estimates implicate the Portuguese in the passage of some 5 million African slaves, and estimates based on records of voyages in the archives of port customs and maritime insurance records put the total number of African slaves transported by European traders to at least 12 million people.

Put simply, the profits accrued from the slave trade helped to finance the Industrial Revolution, and in due course the Caribbean islands grew in significance to become the hub of the British Empire. These sugar colonies were Britain's most valuable overseas assets, contributing by the end of the 18th century some £4 million to the British economy, compared with just £1 million from the rest of the British Empire. The most reliable available statics come from records of the long British involvement in the trans-Atlantic Slave Trade, which formed by far the richest compliment of the British trade economy during the 18th century. During that period, about 70 percent of total British income was derived from taxes on goods from its colonies. The revenues generated by the trans-Atlantic Slave Trade in particular, known as the Triangular Trade, were enormous. These profits derived from the mechanics of the trade itself – direct profits, taxation and of course the export of British and European manufactured goods – but also in relation to the plantation economies that the slave phenomenon itself supported.

The economic effects of the trade of course benefited others besides the traders and plantation owners. A great deal of money was generated amongst those at the primary end of the market, the African kings, monarchs and trading elites who provided the raw materials of the trade, without whom it's scale would never have been possible. The ship building and fitting industries of Europe, in particular Britain, specifically those of Bristol and Liverpool, experienced an unprecedented boom. British factory owners profited handsomely from the trade goods shipped in vast quantities overseas, and which were used by slave captains to barter. An estimated half of the textile production of Manchester was exported to Africa, and half to the West Indies. Birmingham had over 4000 gun-makers, with 100,000 guns a year going to slave-traders. In addition, industrial plants were developed and built in England built to refine the imported raw sugar, and of course glassware was needed to bottle the rum.

A painting depicting a market in the West Indies

The emergence of the British banking industry was factored in no small part upon the profits of slavery, with the entire phenomenon, and its allied phenomenon, jump starting a massive employment boom in Britain and throughout the colonies that established the imperial character of Britain during the 18th and 19th centuries, underwriting the great personal fortunes that were accrued, and creating the capacity for the British Empire to emerge as the greatest formal empire in human history.

By the dawn of the 19th century, following the ban on slave traffic implemented by Britain and the United States, the Atlantic trade began its decline. However, despite this, in the period between the trade ban and full abolition, some trading continued. In fact, about 28 percent of imports took place at this time, with much of the trade still in British hands.

Chapter 3: The Middle Passage

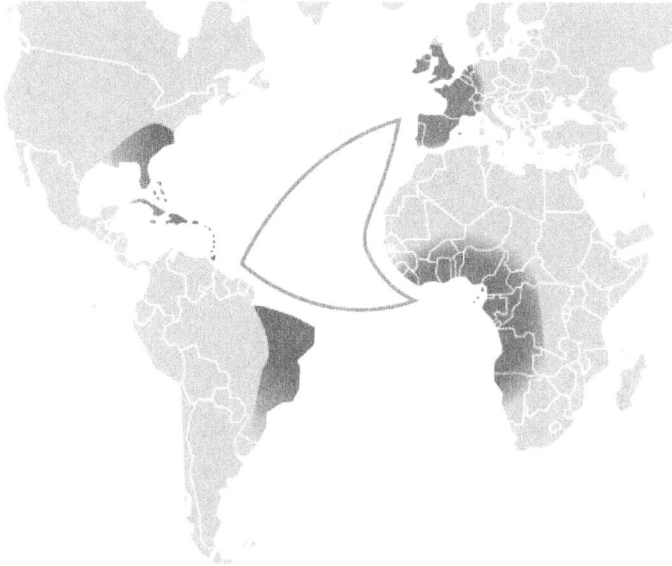

A map of the Transatlantic Slave Trade and Middle Passage

The term Triangular Trade is often heard in contemporary terms in reference to the trans-Atlantic slave trade. The notion of a triangular trade implies a system of trade between three ports, based on the collection and transport of goods required in a third port other than the port of origin. For example, slave ships fitted in Liverpool or Bristol and underwritten by British capital traveled to West Africa in order to acquire slaves, a commodity that was required in the New World, returning to Britain on the third leg laden with high value products such as sugar and tobacco in high demand in Europe. The Middle Passage, therefore, refers to the second leg of this voyage, from the coast of West Africa to the New World across the mid-Atlantic.

William Jackson's painting of a Liverpool slave ship

Much of the iconography of horror and repulsion that has come to influence contemporary memories of the slave trade is associated with the Middle Passage. Slaves were acquired inland of the African coast by one means or another, after which they were mustered and held at various points along the coast as consignments were accumulated for shipment. Most of the established castles and factories such as Cape Coast or Elmina had large holding facilities of one form or another on site to hold captured Africans for varying periods of time. The period involved, of course, could vary, but seldom was it more than a few weeks. There would typically have been a great deal of wastage during this period, with those individuals weakened by the overland march quickly succumbing to cramped and unsanitary conditions. In Cape Coast Castle, for example, the holding dungeons were located partially underground, and without natural light or ventilation. The floors sloped inwards towards a central channel which theoretically would allow human waste to flow out of the dungeon and into the ocean, but overcrowding and decades of constant use had resulted in a layer some feet deep of feces and urine, dried and compacted below but liquid and rancid at the surface. The administrative and living quarters on the upper floors were exceptionally well ventilated, with wide windows to wash out what must have been a perpetual and overpowering smell.

Most of these monuments today have such a thing as a Door of No Return, which is something of a modern nomenclature based on the gates through which slaves would leave the castle or barracoon, to embark onto lighters for the short voyage beyond the breakers, and there to be loaded onto a slave ship, never to return.

Of course, that was just the beginning of the Middle Passage for the slaves. Available statistics offer only a very superficial basis for approximating the numbers of slaves arriving safely in the Americas, but the most authoritative estimates suggest a figure of 12 million. The mortality rate has also historically been a matter of speculation, with 40 percent the most frequently cited figure for early voyages and 10 percent more common towards the end. One writer described a slave ship and the mortality rate: "This ship, though a much smaller ship than in which I have just mentioned, took on board at Bonny at least six hundred Negroes . . . By purchasing so great a number, the slaves were so crowded that they were obliged to lie one upon another. This caused such a mortality among them that without meeting with unusually bad weather or having a longer voyage than common, nearly one half of them died before the ship arrived in the West Indies..."[1] This implies, therefore, that across the board, a high mortality rate was considered acceptable, with the additional advantage of weeding out the weak and sickly early and thus ensuring a robust gene pool of working muscle. It is also indicative of the fact that initially, human cargo was dirt cheap and relatively expendable, at least compared to later stages in the trade when demand had increased and a growing scarcity of available manpower conspired to drive the price up. Cargo was more therefore valuable, and greater effort was expended to preserve it.

Typically, captives would be cleaned and disinfected as much as possible before being carefully examined. Men and women were stripped naked and inspected, their heads were shaved, and the sick or weak were separated out (and often killed shortly after). In certain instances, individuals were branded with the mark of their new owners, who would then be able to recognize them upon arrival. From there, in a state of nakedness, understandably fearing that they had been captured as food, and under the impetus of the whip, they would be herded on board. Crewmen would receive them in manageable batches, packing the holds in a configuration carefully calculated to stow as many individuals as possible.

This was the most dangerous moment of the process, as it would typically be now that those realizing the terminal position that they were in would attempt to rebel. Many such rebellions were recorded, most ending badly for the captives, but some ending badly for the crew too. Others might simply leap overboard, trusting themselves to death rather than captivity. An interesting observation that has been often quoted is that sharks were rare along the West African

[1] Alexander Falconbridge

coast, with the exception of those areas where slaves were processed and embarked. Other accounts observe that sharks frequently followed slave ships for much of the journey, anticipating the jettisoning of both living and dead slaves at various points along the way.

Such incidences did, of course, occur, but it would be with perhaps mundane passivity that a vast majority would bend to the circumstances, enter the hold of the ship, and there, in the darkness and smell, prepare themselves for whatever fate might lie in wait for them. According to one of the few available first hand narratives, this one composed by Olaudah Equiano, Every circumstance served only to heighten my....opinion of the cruelty of the whites. One day they had taken fishes; and when they had satisfied themselves with as many as they thought fit...rather than give any of them to us to eat...they tossed the remaining fish into the sea again. [Once] when we had a smooth sea and moderate wind, two of my wearied countrymen who were chained together, preferring death to a life of misery somehow made through the [deck] netting and jumped into the sea; immediately another fellow followed their example; and I believe many more would very soon have done the same, if they had not been prevented by the ship's crew. Two of the wretches were drowned, but they got the other and afterwards flogged him unmercifully for attempting to prefer death to slavery.[2]

---

[2] Olaudah Equiano, 1745 – 31 March, 1797, known in later life as *Gustavus Vassa* was a prominent African and freedom advocate who was based in London. He was a freed slave, and his autobiography, published in 1789 attracted wide attention. Equiano is regarded as having been highly influential in gaining passage of the *Slave Trade Act 1807*, which ended the African trade for Britain and its colonies.

Olaudah Equiano,
or
GUSTAVUS VASSA,
the African?

Equiano

The Middle Passage was facilitated by the Atlantic's prevailing winds and ocean currents, which formed giant "wheels" north and south of the equator. These facilitated the three-way movement of trade, but they also made the Atlantic crossing very difficult. Long diversions south were necessary before turning northwest and passing through the doldrums, and as a consequence, although some voyages were recorded at just a few weeks, others could take months.

As the trade progressed, sailing technology improved, cutting passage times significantly, but the rigors of the experience for those chained in ship holds almost defy imagination. Olaudah Equiano recalled, "I was soon put down under the decks, and there I received such a salutation in my nostrils as I had never experienced in my life: So that, with the loathsomeness of stench, and with my crying together, I became so sick and low that I was not able to eat, nor had I the least desire to taste anything…"

A typical storage system involved what were known as apartments, which were in effect platforms extending inward from the sides of the hold with a central passage for movement. These typically offered three feet of vertical space, making it impossible for individual slaves to stand. Movement was also complicated by the fact that individuals were often shackled to one another and closely compacted, making it difficult and painful to shift sides or attempt to move. Most would be naked, and of course the availability of any kind of ablution would be very limited.

A very strong description of conditions on board a slave ship was offered by the personal account of Dr. Alexander Falconbridge, a British surgeon who participated in a handful of slave ship voyages in the 1780s. He later became a leading abolitionist, and in 1788 he published *An Account of the Slave Trade on the Coast of Africa*, which would emerge as a seminal work that influenced the abolitionist movement. According to Falconbridge, slaves barely had room to do anything besides lay on the floor: "But at the same time, however, they are frequently stowed so close, as to admit of no other position than lying on their sides. Nor will the height between decks, unless directly under the grating, permit the indulgence of an erect posture; especially where there are platforms, which is generally the case. These platforms are a kind of shelf, about eight or nine feet in breadth, extending from the side of the ship toward the centre. They are placed nearly midway between the decks, at the distance of two or three feet from each deck, Upon these the Negroes are stowed in the same manner as they are on the deck underneath."

In the few available accounts of conditions aboard slave ships, it is noted that there would typically be some accommodation made for latrines. This would usually amount to a small apartment separated from the main hold containing one or more tubs. Access to these would naturally be very difficult, bearing in mind that slaves were usually shackled to one another, and one can easily imagine that under those conditions, attempting to detach oneself in order to access a tub would result in the irritation and discomfort of others, which would have resulted in disturbances and quarrels.

Most frequently, individuals would simply relieve themselves where they sat, to the obvious consternation of those seated below, and given the heat of the tropics and the lack of ventilation, the conditions would begin very quickly to result in endemic gastrointestinal diseases and a range of epidemic pathogens that, along with the comparatively mundane experience of seasickness, would have contributed not only to the awful discomfort of those suffering but also to the overall mortality rate. According to Olaudah Equiano, "The closeness of the place, and the heat of the climate, added to the number in the ship, which was so crowded that each had scarcely room to turn himself, almost suffocated us. This produced copious perspirations, so that the air soon became unfit for respiration, from a variety of loathsome smells and brought on a sickness among the slaves of which many died."

Among those feared gastrointestinal maladies, perhaps the most dreaded was dysentery, which is highly contagious and was known as bloody flux. Dysentery is defined by the Oxford English Dictionary as "an abnormally copious flowing of blood and excrement from the bowels or other organs; a morbid or excessive discharge." With the limited availability of water, dehydration was inevitable, and certain accounts claim dehydration to be the chief cause of mortality.

Under these circumstances, it's easy to imagine the effect of an epidemic of dysentery on board the ship, along with other feared conditions such as smallpox and scurvy. Falconbridge wrote, "Some wet and blowing weather having occasioned the port-holes to be shut and the grating to be covered, fluxes and fevers among the Negroes ensued. While they were in this situation, I frequently went down among them till at length their room became so extremely hot as to be only bearable for a very short time. But the excessive heat was not the only thing that rendered their situation intolerable. The deck, that is the floor of their rooms, was so covered with the blood and mucus which had proceeded from them in consequence of the flux, that it resembled a slaughter-house. It is not in the power of the human imagination to picture a situation more dreadful or disgusting. Numbers of the slaves having fainted, they were carried upon deck where several of them died and the rest with great difficulty were restored. It had nearly proved fatal to me also. The climate was too warm to admit the wearing of any clothing but a shirt and that I had pulled off before I went down.... In a quarter of an hour I was so overcome with the heat, stench and foul air that I nearly fainted, and it was only with assistance I could get back on deck. The consequence was that I soon after fell sick of the same disorder from which I did not recover for several months..."

Depending on the ship and the circumstances, slaves might be allowed to sojourn on deck for periods of time, albeit still shackled in large numbers, and rotated with others below. Still, their poor diets were not sufficient or varied enough to sustain health.

Perhaps not surprisingly, discipline on board was swift and predictably brutal, with a variety of methods employed, most notably floggings. These methods, actual or implied, lived with slaves as a fact of life throughout the entire passage, and in many cases beyond. In conjunction with that, women often had to endure being raped by owners or captors as part of the reality of living utterly devoid of rights.

As an unintended consequence of the trauma of the Middle Passage, slaves, when finally landfall was made, would be so weakened, terrorized and demoralized that any further resistance to their fate would be very improbable. Within sight of land, they would usually given access to better food and fortified as much as possible before disembarkation. There would typically be a great sense of anxiety felt about the future, with a majority of slaves anticipating that they had been sold to be eaten, so they were convinced that this would be the moment. Quite often, older Creole slaves would be brought on board to pacify this fear, explaining to the newcomers that many of their countrymen were waiting on land for them and that henceforth they would be expected simply to work.

On land, the dying were separated from the firm and thereafter sold cheaply to speculators who afterwards attempted to revive them in the hope of bring them up to a saleable condition. Others would very quickly find themselves at an auction or some such other market or exchange, where they would be bought or in some other way claimed. Dr. Falconbridge made note of a system of sale known as the Scramble: "In a scramble, each slave is priced the same and the slave-desperate buyers were allowed to purchase all they could claim. Upon a given signal, or time, the purchasers would race into the holding pin and grab or lay claim to the best and healthiest. Sometimes they would encircle whole groupings with a rope. Determined to get the best, arguments and fights would break out between the competitive purchasers."

In the entire pantheon of horrors that attended the Atlantic Slave Trade, the rigors of the Middle Passage arguably rank the worst. Naturally, it was people like Alexander Falconbridge and John Newton who emerged as the most passionate and vocal supporters of abolition after they had witnessed these dehumanizing circumstances for long periods.[3]

---

[3] Note: John Newton was an English sailor, serving first in the Royal Navy, and later a captain of slave ships. He became ordained as an evangelical Anglican cleric, also wrote hymns, known for *Amazing Grace* and *Glorious Things of Thee are Spoken*. He later became an abolitionist.

Depiction of a sugarcane plantation

Upon their arrival, the slaves' experience in the new world varied very much according to location and the circumstances under which each individual slave found himself or herself. Generally speaking, slavery in the New World had an industrial flavor that ancient systems of slavery did not; certainly in the African context, slavery had long existed, but it did so under loosely defined conventions, and usually in terms of war booty or as a response to criminality of some sort or another. Slaves were held within established traditions of society and utilized principally within concubinage or domestic service, with some defined term of bondage that ended at a certain point or with manumission offered under certain conditions. At no time in history prior to the advent of the Transatlantic slave trade was slavery regarded as an economic phenomenon, similar to the way fossil fuels or electricity might now be regarded as a source of expendable agricultural or economic power.

The history of the New World economies and the history of slavery are inseparable from one another, and each are associated primarily with the production of sugar, cotton and tobacco. It is a fact that the aboriginal peoples of the Americas withered away almost at the moment that white contact with their land mass took place. This happened mostly because of the introduction of exotic disease and alcohol than the predations of slavery, and furthermore, Native Americans were emotionally and physically unsuited to the style of labor that the Portuguese demanded as they began to establish the first commercial sugar plantations in Brazil. Even without alcohol and disease, it would seem unlikely that the Europeans would have ever considered any indigenous society as a viable source of labor.

Europe was introduced to sugar by the Arabs in the 15th century, which coincided with the Portuguese and Spanish advances in Africa and the Americas. The commodity was well received, quite naturally, after which a market was formed and rapidly grew. Sugar was at first grown among the Mediterranean islands, but demand so quickly began to exceed supply that the crop was established in Brazil, Cuba, Mexico and the Caribbean as well. This prompted the rapid growth of a plantation economy that attracted not only Iberian immigrant farmers but also British, French and Dutch farmers. As the industry grew, so did the importation of slave labor.

In terms of the conditions that greeted new arrivals in the Americas, these varied with destination. However, the dehumanizing process that had begun on the African mainland, and which was reinforced by the conditions of the Middle Passage, was usually refined considerably at the point of sale. This dehumanization, however, as brutally as it was applied to those victims of the slave trade, also applied in many respects to those engaged in the trade. If dehumanization is necessary in order to justify the commitment of atrocities against individuals, a nation or an entire race, then it stands to reason that a certain amount of dehumanization will affect those wielding the force within that social equation.

A depiction of slaves being punished in Rio de Janeiro

The removal of personal identity and individuality was achieved (albeit probably by happenstance) to a large degree by the random mingling of people of diverse cultures and language groups into a single homogenous mass. Ultimately, slaves were forced by a lack of any common medium of communication to adopt the language of their oppressors, evolving invariably into a style of pidgin, and to be renamed, adopting either the names of their new owners or some codified system of naming that separated them from their original identity.

All of this, and a great deal more besides, permitted black slaves to be regarded as commodities, with the application of brutal methods of coercion simply the necessary means of controlling and applying the labor of a large number of people who would otherwise be capable, with sufficient impetus and organization, of overrunning a generally smaller and practically vulnerable class of owners.

Only about 5 percent of slaves exported out of Africa between 1501 and 1866 were absorbed by British North America. This amounts to approximately 500,000 out of the estimated 12,500,000 embarked (10,700,000 disembarked, implying a death rate of some 14.52 percent), with increases thereafter being through natural increase.

This then introduces the question of the status and conditioning of slave progeny, the only practical means of renewing numbers in the British sphere after the outlawing of the trade in 1808. Bearing in mind the singular lack of first person narratives to emerge from the institution of slavery in the New World, one is forced often to rely on the few that did emerge, such as those written by Frederick Douglass and Booker T. Washington, the former of whom escaped slavery and the latter released from slavery at the conclusion of the Civil War. According to Frederick Douglass, at the moment of birth, the child of a slave mother was removed from her care. As he explained, the purpose of this was to "hinder the development of the child's affection towards its mother, and to blunt and destroy the natural affection of the mother for the child. This is the inevitable result."[4] Birthdates were withheld, family units were disassembled, and literacy and education universally denied. The powerlessness of an individual in a situation where no capital or financial system existed, no education and no social support structures were permitted, and there were no legal rights of any sort is hard to comprehend in the modern world.[5] Indeed, one of the greatest challenges facing African Americans after the passing of the 13th and 14th Amendment was the establishment of the fundamental institutions necessary for the entry into mainstream life of hundreds of thousands of recently emancipated blacks. These were now part of the mainstream cash economy, and abruptly denied the support mechanisms, if such can be described, of a system that had oppressed them, but nonetheless, in general terms, had also provided for them.[6]

Conditions in North America remained relatively benign compared to conditions in Brazil and much of the Caribbean. Between 60 and 70 percent of Africans exported across Atlantic ended up either in Brazil or the sugar colonies of the Caribbean, and yet by 1860 approximately two thirds of all New World slaves lived in the American South.[7] What this statistic implies at the very least is a shocking mortality rate of slave labor in the Spanish and Portuguese colonies and the British sugar islands. Prior to the advent of detailed studies, there had been a general assumption that the ubiquity of the Catholic Church in the Spanish and Portuguese colonies tended to ameliorate the worst excesses of treatment against those subject to slavery. Slaves, for example, enjoyed the right to marry and could seek a certain amount of institutionalized relief against cruel overlordship or unacceptably harsh conditions. It was also assumed that Spanish and Portuguese colonists were less subjected to the petty racial prejudices that so characterized white attitudes north of the Isthmus of Panama.

In theory all of this was true, but in practice somewhat less so. The Catholic Church can reflect on a long and questionable history of upholding and protecting human rights, and while

---

[4] *Narrative of the Life of Frederick Douglass.*

[5] Note: Before the fourteenth amendment to the national constitution (July 28, 1868), blacks held no legal rights in the United States.

[6] Note: After the outlawing of the slave trade, and prior to the abolition of the institution of slavery in the United States, it became necessary to utilize natural reproduction as a means of replenishing numbers, and so a more humane system began to evolve, with greater emphasis placed on improved living and working conditions in order to discourage escape or abandonment.

[7] Source: *Gilder Lehrman Institute of American History*

Portuguese and Spanish colonists were certainly able to claim a greater degree of racial tolerance in terms of social integration and interrelationship, the Portuguese in particular had a lamentable record of human rights within their colonies and were among the last of the European powers to recognize the inevitability of independence amongst their subject colonies.

Slave mortality in the Caribbean in general was about a third higher than in the Southern states of the U.S., and suicide appears, statistically at least, to have been a very real factor.[8] A very common policy in the Caribbean was the requirement that slaves produce their own food alongside their labor obligations, and to provide care for those vulnerable amongst them such as the ill, young or elderly.

Perhaps most interesting, however, is the differences between gender rations in Brazil and the West Indies compared to the South. In the case of the former, the proportion of female slaves was much lower, with consequently lower birthrates, and the requirement therefore to augment losses and satisfy increased demand with ongoing imports. In contrast, the United States hosted a fairly equal distribution of male and female slaves, with higher birthrates and an almost total American-born slave population by the middle of the 18th century.

There were also other, more subtle differences between the two systems. Abuse, violence and brutality were not as universally prevalent in the Southern United States as popular mythology might imply. Certain immutable rules applied to owner/slave relationships, and so long as these rules were respected, it can be taken for granted that a majority of slave owners treated their chattel with a similar degree of humanity and respect as might be applied to any human relationship, with adjustments to class and race considered. Brutality existed on the fringes of the institution, and extreme brutality on the outer fringes, as one can perhaps easily imagine in a situation where one class enjoys absolute power over another. For those with an appetite for such thing, cruelty and abuse against blacks was legal, and some certainly availed themselves of the privilege.

A very different set of circumstances existed in the West Indies, where plantations were strictly commercial in character. Sugar tended to be the crop of choice, and the rigors and labor intensity of sugar production immediately introduced an extra layer of difficulty for Caribbean slaves. In the West Indies, European planters were outnumbered by slaves by about 8-1, and indeed many of these were practically absentee landlords who relied on a class of free black overseers to manage most aspects of production and labor management in their absence. Few questions were ever asked, and in a vacuum of regulation or oversight, slaves existed as a very expendable commodity that proved cheaper to replace than sustain.

Chapter 5: Abolition

"It is so odious, that nothing can be suffered to support it, but positive law." – William Murray, 1st Earl of Mansfield

All the European nations in one way or another were implicit in the factoring and utilization of

---

[8] *Ibid.*

slave labor, if not directly then at least through a growing appetite for commodities produced by slave labor. However, with the advent of mass communications and the general perceptiveness of the European population, by the end of the 18th century there was in existence a well-established undercurrent of social unease in relation to the slave trade. This coincided in broad terms with the advent of steam power and the rapid industrialization of Europe that followed.

In this regard, once again, a parallel might perhaps profitably be drawn between human power and fossil fuels. Quite as the world population of today recognizes that fossil fuels are unsustainable and responsible primarily for ongoing climate change, in the absence of any alternative millions still fill up the gas tanks. Such was slavery during the 19th century, and it was only upon the gradual introduction of alternative methods of industrial power that options for its actual abolition became feasible. However, such as one might recognize today, powerful vested interests prevailed for a very long time. Nonetheless, the general social mood in Europe began to become increasingly hostile towards slavery and progressively more receptive to the voice of the abolitionist movement.

Abolition is a very broad term encompassing many diverse threads that coalesced only in the first decades of the 19th century into a movement of international reach. The first awareness began to seep into European institutionalized thinking with the Age of Enlightenment. During the 17th century, philosophers began to argue reason and empiricism over religious dogma, culminating in the ideas of philosophers and thinkers such as Voltaire, Descartes, Francis Bacon and Sir Isaac Newton. The concept of individual rights and freedoms began to emerge at this time, culminating in the great global milestone of the enlightenment period: The French Revolution.

Fittingly, it was in France that the first legislation dealing specifically with slavery was enacted. In the year 1315, King Louis X of France declared mainland France free of slavery. This was followed by a 1685 decree issued by Louis XIV of France codifying a general law governing the conditions of slavery in the French colonial empire. It also limited the freedoms and liberties of freed blacks and ordered the expulsion of all Jews from French overseas territories. This was the Code Noir, or Black Code, and on the question of overseas slavery it offered certain rights to individuals, including the right to marry, to demonstrate, and to take time off. However, it also mandated severe forms of punishment, only partially ameliorated somewhat by strict provisos against torture and the separation of families. A key clause of these decrees also mandated instruction in the Catholic faith, which was a major symbolic advance insofar as for the first time it elevated black slaves to the status of a human being possessing a soul.

In 1792, the French government granted the rights of full French citizenship to all freed men of color, and on February 4, 1794, slavery was abolished in law in France and its colonies. This proved to be something of a test case for the maturity of the abolition movement, because no sooner had the law been enacted than a virtual mutiny occurred among French overseas sugar and general commodity producers, who threatened to take their colonies over to the British (under whom slavery remained legal). The British, of course, would have made such rebels most welcome under the Pax Britannia. Thus, Napoleon Bonaparte, concerned more with the cohesion of the empire than the finer moral points of emancipation, promulgated the law of May 20, 1802, reviving slavery and sending military governors and troops to the colonies to impose it.[9]

This news prompted a series of French slave rebellions, culminating in the French withdrawal from the island of Saint-Domingue and the birth of the independent island republic of Haiti in 1804. It also helped prompt the sale of the territory of Louisiana to the United States, and a general drawing in of French interests overseas. On April 27, 1848, under the Second Republic, a decree-law abolished slavery in the remaining French overseas dependencies. Slaves were thereafter purchased by the state and freed.

The British may have been slower to start, but they were without a doubt the first nation over the finish line, with the full abolition of slavery throughout the British Empire codified under law in 1838. The preamble to this achievement reflected Britain's preeminence in Europe at that time; it was only once the British had weighed in that the international institution of slavery came under its first real threat.

Possibly the greatest irony of the period of slavery was the fact that the British refined and perfected the Transatlantic trade to a greater extent than any other nation, and profited from it to a gargantuan degree, while at the same time allowing the seeds of the abolitionist movement to flourish no less vigorously. As the nation with the greatest naval and merchant fleets, it was this dominance of the world's oceans that first gave Britain such a great advantage is prosecuting the trade, and later the power and authority to enforce its abolition.

Britain could claim no specific, codified domestic law that stated any position on slavery within the Kingdom at all, but a precedent was established as early as 1569 when an English court ruled that a slave imported from Russia could not be held as such since slavery had never been formally introduced into England and thus did not technically exist. This was followed up much later by a landmark 1700 ruling that determined that a slave became free at the moment that he set foot on English soil. Two years later, in 1772, Lord Mansfield, Chief Justice of the King's Bench, rendered slavery unenforceable at common law through a decision that has since been regarded as one of major turning points in the formation of the abolition movement. It reads in part as follows, "The state of slavery is of such a nature, that it is incapable of being introduced on any reasons, moral or political; but only positive law, which preserves its force long after the reasons, occasion, and time itself from whence it was created, is erased from memory: it's so odious, that nothing can be suffered to support it, but positive law. Whatever inconveniences, therefore, may follow from a decision, I cannot say this case is allowed or approved by the law of England; and therefore the black must be discharged."[10]

---

[9] Note: The Law of 20 May 1802 was a French law passed on 20 May 1802, revoking the law of 4 February 1794 which had abolished slavery in all the French colonies.

[10] *Affect and Abolition in the Anglo-Atlantic*, 1770-1830, edited by Stephen Ahern, (Ashgate Publishing Ltd, England 2013) p77

Lord Mansfield

What this implied at the time was that an institution that impacts the human condition as gravely as slavery cannot be allowed to exist until legislation allows, if ever, and thus that's the way it was dealt with in England and Wales. For the colonies of the British Empire, however, where a vast majority of slaves resided, the institution of slavery and the trade in slaves remained legal.

It was not until the founding and organization of the Society for the Abolition of the Slave Trade in May of 1787 that the consolidation of British efforts towards the abolition of slavery began to gather genuine momentum. This group took the most active lead in creating general awareness through the publication dissemination of books, pamphlets and other literature that highlighted the horrors of the slave trade and built a general constituency around the issue. The London chapter was supported by regional subcommittees and agents who provided an active link between London, the counties, and a great many emerging grass roots activist groups.

Image on an abolitionist medallion

A late 18th century medallion advocating abolition

William Wilberforce, a British parliamentarian, was recruited to the movement in order to lead the charge in the House of Commons, which he did. This proved, arguably, to be the decisive factor as a series of petition campaigns, including all told some 519 petitions, revealed a degree of diversity and range of opposition to slavery. It was a campaign that almost succeeded when in 1792 the British House of Commons resolved to adopt a phased abolition throughout the Empire, a ruling which was unfortunately revisited the following year and reversed in the light of unfolding events in revolutionary France.

Wilberforce

The American Revolution also facilitated the growth of an anti-slavery movement. "As long as America was ours," wrote abolitionist Thomas Clarkson in 1788, "there was no chance that a minister would have attended to the groans of the sons and daughters of Africa, however he might feel for their distress."

This global uncertainty, however, revealed itself to be the very catalyst required for accelerated change. The acquisition by Britain of a number of new territories in the West Indies as a consequence of the dispensations of the Napoleonic Wars, notably Trinidad, Berbice, and Demerara, created a great deal of anxiety among the original British settler elite regarding the possibility of enhanced competition, which acted to drive them into the arms of the abolition movement. Capitalizing on this revised position in the Caribbean, and the entry into Parliament of a number of liberal Irish MPs, the abolitionists in 1804 renewed their campaign. In 1805 a Bill providing for the abolition of the slave trade to newly acquired territories, most notably in the Caribbean, was tabled, successfully passing through both Houses in 1807 and being implemented in 1808.

Thereafter, the target became the abolition of the institution of slavery in its entirety. Soon after that signature 1807 victory, the British Society for the Abolition of the Slave Trade was superseded by the African Institution, a pressure group whose objective was to ensure the adequate enforcement of anti-slavery legislation and to lobby for a more general, international commitment to abolition. It is perhaps interesting to note that one of the areas of interest of the African Institution was the settlement of the city of Freetown, the main coastal port of the British African territory of Sierra Leone.

The territory of Sierra Leone was founded by the British as a Crown dependency in 1792. The territory had been established primarily for the resettlement of freed slaves, first from Britain itself, and then from the North American mainland. From 1808-1874, Freetown served as both the capital of British West Africa and the base for the Royal Navy's West Africa Squadron, which was the naval force mandated to implement the British ban on the trade in slaves. Slaves liberated during blockade operations were frequently resettled in Freetown and surroundings, creating a uniquely homogeneous population that frequently clashed with indigenous societies. The British also established six internationally located Mixed Courts for the purpose of enforcing the ban, three of which (Anglo-Portuguese, Anglo-Spanish and Anglo-Dutch courts) were based in Sierra Leone.

The Royal Naval West Africa Squadron fined captains transporting slaves £120 per slave carried, and by 1865, nearly 150,000 people freed by anti-slavery operations. At the height of its operations, the squadron employed a sixth of the Royal Navy fleet and marines. Until 1835, the Royal Navy was only allowed to take slavers that actually had slaves aboard. This meant the squadron could not interfere with vessels clearly equipped for the trade but without a cargo, which gave slavers being pursued an incentive to throw their slaves overboard before capture to avoid the seizure of the vessel.

Britain also actively pressed other nations into treaties to give the Royal Navy the right to search their ships for slaves. As the 19th century wore on, the Royal Navy began interdicting slave trading in North Africa, the Middle East, and the Indian Ocean.

A depiction of a Royal Navy ship stopping a slave trader

The U.S. followed the British lead in 1808 by banning the trade in slaves throughout America, but it left the institution of slavery itself largely legal and entrenched throughout the world. By then, however, the tide had effectively turned, and in piecemeal form the pillars of the intuition were beginning to crumble. In 1810, Mexico abolished slavery in its mainland territories, and the following year Spain abolished slavery at home and in all colonies except Cuba, Puerto Rico, and Santo Domingo. The same year Chile declared the iconic Freedom of Wombs, prohibiting the slave trade and freeing the sons of slaves born on Chilean territory.[11] The Freedom of Wombs then became law in Argentina in 1813, followed by Uruguay a year later. In 1814, the Dutch Government outlawed the slave trade

This process continued as a general outlawing of the trade in slaves gathered momentum amongst all of the world's major powers, as well as a great many minor powers. Various treaties of cooperation were signed between Britain and other erstwhile participating powers to cooperate in enforcing an international ban on trade. The first instances of slavery in its entirety being outlawed in an English speaking territory was probably the 1819 declaration in the province of Upper Canada that all black residents of the territory were henceforth free.[12] Thereafter, Mexico

---

[11] Note: *The Law*, or *Freedom of the Wombs* was a judicial principle applied in several countries in South America in the 19th century, freeing the children of slaves at birth, removing them as property of the parents' owners.

[12] Note: The Province of *Upper Canada* was established in 1791 by the United Kingdom to govern the central third of the lands in British North

abolished slavery, followed by Chile, which then set the tone for the establishment of the British Anti-Slavery Society in 1823.

That group signaled an all-out assault against the international institution of slavery itself. The Anti-Slavery Society was supported by a great many powerful voices in the British political establishment, including prominent abolitionists such as Thomas Clarkson and William Wilberforce. Intense lobbying, alongside commissions of inquiry to establish the causes of a major slave rebellion in 1831 that broke out on the island of Jamaica, reached an inevitable climax in 1833 with the passing of a landmark act in the British House of Commons: the Abolition of Slavery Act, which in practical terms set the tone for the rest of the world.

The greatest resistance to full abolition was, of course, felt and registered in the United States, to the extent that it was the main cause of the Civil War. The American Revolution had transferred the moral question of slavery and all its ramifications from Britain to the American colonies themselves, and many of the Founding Fathers, such as the slaveowner Thomas Jefferson, pushed for abolitionist stances but realized the pragmatism of compromise. Jefferson, indeed, supported the Missouri Compromise of 1820, enacted in the same year that Mexico wholly abolished the institution.[13]

On the eve of the Civil War, as the United States was growing and calls for abolition following the British act growing louder and louder by the moment, slavery remained entrenched in the plantation regions of the South. The abolition movement at that time was focused in the North and was organized under the umbrella of the American Anti-Slavery Society, led by such reformists as William Lloyd Garrison (who founded the Society) and writers and activists like John Greenleaf Whittier and Harriet Beecher Stowe. Active also were a large and growing number of black activists such as former slave Frederick Douglass.

America and to accommodate Loyalist refugees of the United States of America after the American Revolution. The new province remained, for the next fifty years of growth and settlement, the colonial government of the territory.

[13] Note: The *Missouri Compromise* was a federal statute in the United States that regulated slavery in the country's western territories, thereby allowing the growth and spread of slavery within the emerging nation.

Douglass

Warren's

Garrison

The moment of crisis came with the 1860 presidential victory of Abraham Lincoln, at which point various Deep South states opted to secede and form a new nation. [14] Eventually, the Civil

---

[14] The seven states that seceded from the United States, and which originally formed the Confederate States of America, were, in order of

War broke out in April 1861, and in 1863 President Lincoln issued the Emancipation Proclamation, which freed all slaves held in the Confederate States. The 13th Amendment to the U.S. Constitution took effect in December 1865, finally ending slavery throughout the United States.[15]

Chapter 6: The Legacy of the Transatlantic Slave Trade

The period of Reconstruction and the evolution of the Civil Rights movement marked the beginning of the long struggle within the United States for some reconciliation between the races after the traumatic experience of slavery. This chapter of American history cannot easily be defined in a few words, and the legacy of the trans-Atlantic Slave Trade on the continent of Africa has always been just as hard to define.

The abolition of slavery in Africa, the embers of which were really not stamped out entirely until the turn of the 20th century, became in large measure the raison d'être for greater European penetration into Africa and the eventual phenomenon of the Scramble for Africa. For example, the formation of the Congo Free State during the closing decades of the 19th century was underwritten by European determination to eradicate the practice on the continent entirely, notwithstanding the eventual perversion of the those principals.

By the first decade of the 20th century, Western style rule of law had been established over most of the continent of Africa, and the large-scale practice of slavery had effectively passed into history. Deep scars remained, however, with vast regions of Africa depopulated and a great many once cohesive societies shattered and destroyed. It is debatable whether the continent ever recovered from such a wholesale looting of its population, with many tending to ascribe the current problems facing Africa as a long-term legacy of this social cataclysm. Additional difficulties have been thrown up by the role of Africans themselves in the slave trade, with only limited willingness on the continent itself to accept that the African slave trade, although facilitated by European trading powers, was monopolized on the continent itself by indigenous players, amongst whom great fortunes were made.

The day has yet to dawn when the deep ripples of both the Atlantic and Indian Ocean Slave Trades will subside and die, but what is inescapable is that this was one of the greatest crimes against humanity ever perpetrated, and that its legacy remains persistent is perhaps ultimately to the benefit of mankind. The term humanitarian disaster is, of course, a modern phrase that has been all too frequently applicable to Africa in recent years. However, there has rarely been an African humanitarian disaster on such a scale as that created by the slave trade, in particular those African individuals, societies and cultures that suffered (and still suffer) as collateral damage.

One of the earliest and most celebrated of the great African explorers was Dr. David Livingstone, who from the 1840s to the early 1870s witnessed and documented the vast human

---

secession: South Carolina, Mississippi, Florida, Alabama, Georgia, Louisiana, and Texas.

[15] Note: The *Thirteenth Amendment to the United States Constitution* abolished slavery and involuntary servitude, except as punishment for a crime.

dislocation and social collapse that had accompanied the predations of slavery, and almost single-handedly brought the issue to the attention of the Victorian public, precipitating much of the movement towards general abolition. Livingstone's primary interest was in the East African or Indian Ocean Slave Trade, which was separate from the Transatlantic slave trade, but it is worth noting that the Indian Ocean trade, although never quite so concentrated as the Atlantic trade, began earlier and survived for much longer. In fact, it was responsible ultimately for the exportation of many more human beings out of Africa (18-21 million according to some estimates). These were mostly destined for markets in the Arabian Peninsula, the Persian Gulf and the Indian Ocean islands.

It also has generally been agreed that the East Africa trade was significantly more destructive to the continent of Africa itself, with unreliable estimates suggesting that for every individual successfully traded on the east coast, three died en route. That doesn't even include the additional attrition and massive loss of life in the interior caused by the violence among warlords and the damage associated with the capture of slaves.

This branch of the trade was dominated by Arab and Indian traders, operating under the administration of the Sultanate of Zanzibar and in cooperation with black, Swahili speaking middlemen who collectively despoiled a vast region of the interior from the coast of Mozambique to Somalia, and as far inland as the eastern edges of the Congo Basin. This branch of the African Slave Trade, which lay almost entirely in non-European hands, proved to be the most difficult to eradicate. The Sultanate of Zanzibar, which had familial relations with the Sultanate of Oman, remained, until the end of the 19th century, a sovereign and independent entity that controlled nearly the entire Swahili speaking portion of the African mainland. It successfully resisted all European pressure to outlaw the trade in slaves, which for millennia had formed an important cornerstone of the Zanzibari and Indian Ocean trade economy.

The East African Slave Trade was only legally outlawed in 1873, upon the signing of a treaty to that effect between the British Government and the Sultan of Zanzibar. This, however, did not immediately bring an end to the human rights abuses and insecurity in the interior of Africa, which continued largely unabated under the ivory trade until effective European occupation of the continent resulted in comprehensive policing and the imposition of rule of law.

Online Resources

Other books about slavery by Charles River Editors

Other books about the slave trade on Amazon

Bibliography

Anstey, Roger: The Atlantic Slave Trade and British Abolition, 1760–1810. London: Macmillan, 1975. ISBN 0-333-14846-0.

Blackburn, Robin (2011). The American Crucible: Slavery, Emancipation and Human Rights. London & New York: Verso. ISBN 978-1-84467-569-2.

Curtin, Philip D.: The Atlantic Slave Trade. University of Wisconsin Press, 1969.

Drescher, Seymour: From Slavery to Freedom: Comparative Studies in the Rise and Fall of Atlantic Slavery. London: Macmillan Press, 1999. ISBN 0-333-73748-2.

Gleeson, David T. and Simon Lewis (eds). Ambiguous Anniversary: The Bicentennial of the International Slave Trade Bans (University of South Carolina Press; 2012) 207 pp.

Hall, Gwendolyn Midlo: Slavery and African Ethnicities in the Americas: Restoring the Links. Chapel Hill, N.C.: The University of North Carolina Press, 2006. ISBN 0-8078-2973-0.

Horne, Gerald: The Deepest South: The United States, Brazil, and the African Slave Trade. New York, NY: New York University Press, 2007. ISBN 978-0-8147-3688-3, ISBN 978-0-8147-3689-0.

Klein, Herbert S.: The Atlantic Slave Trade (2nd edn, 2010).

Lindsay, Lisa A. "Captives as Commodities: The Transatlantic Slave Trade". Prentice Hall, 2008. ISBN 978-0-13-194215-8

Meltzer, Milton: Slavery: A World History. New York: Da Capo Press, 1993. ISBN 0-306-80536-7.

Northrup, David: The Atlantic Slave Trade (3rd edn, 2010)

Rediker, Marcus (2007). The Slave Ship: A Human History. New York, NY: Viking Press. ISBN 978-0-670-01823-9.

Rodney, Walter: How Europe Underdeveloped Africa. Washington, D.C.: Howard University Press; Revised edn, 1981. ISBN 0-88258-096-5.

Solow, Barbara (ed.), Slavery and the Rise of the Atlantic System. Cambridge: Cambridge University Press, 1991. ISBN 0-521-40090-2.

Thomas, Hugh: The Slave Trade: The History of the Atlantic Slave Trade 1440–1870. London: Picador, 1997. ISBN 0-330-35437-X.; comprehensive history

Printed in Great Britain
by Amazon

49115390R00031